Revised edition published 1982
By The People of God
P.O. Box 16406
Nairobi, Kenya

Reprinted 2015

Cover photo credit: Caleb Bornman

# The People of Faith

## More Lessons

## from

## The Holy Scriptures

## Course Four

# The People of Faith

Welcome to this course called: **The People of Faith**

You have been a good student. You have finished three courses in the Scripture study series which is called **The People of God.** These are the courses you have completed:

**1. The Beginning of People**
This course was from the first book of the **Taurat.**

**2. God's Covenant with People**
This course was from the second book of the **Taurat**, from the **Zabur**, and from the book of the Prophet Isaiah.

**3. God Loves people**
This course was from the **Injil.**

Now you are ready for the last course in this series. This last course is called **The People of Faith**. There are five lessons in this course. Each lesson is taken from the New Testament of the Bible. These lessons will show you what the People of God believe and do.

We wish you great success in this last course! And we pray that God will bless you.

# Lesson 1

## The Church

Before you do this lesson, read these verses from the Bible:      Acts 2:1-47
Acts 9: 1-22
Ephesians 4: 4-6

Now read the lesson and do the test at the end. The lesson explains what you have read in the Bible.

---

The Christian Church is the fellowship of people who have answered the call of God to accept the Messiah as their Saviour and Lord. The Church began ten days after Jesus the Messiah returned to Heaven.

### The Beginning of the Church (Acts 2: 1-47)

After Jesus the Messiah rose from the dead, he told his disciples to be his witnesses, first in Jerusalem, then in Palestine and finally to the whole world (Acts 1:8). But first he told his disciples to wait in Jerusalem until the Holy Spirit came upon them (Acts 1:4-5).

---

People who have studied the Quran know that the Quran teaches many things about the Holy Spirit of God. In Surat Al-Hijr (15) ayah 29 we read about the creation of man: "When I have made him (man) and have breathed my Spirit in him, you (angels) fall down prostrating before him."

The Quran also speaks of God sending his Spirit to Mary so that she could give birth to the Messiah (Surat Maryam (19) ayah 17; Surat Al-Anbiya (21) ayah 91).

The Quran also calls the Messiah a Spirit from God (Surat An-Nisa (4): ayah 171) and said that God supported the Messiah by the Holy Spirit (Surat Al-Baqarah (2) ayah 253 and Surat Al-Ma'idah (5) ayah 110).

---

**After the Messiah returned to heaven, the disciples and others of Jesus' followers obeyed Jesus by staying in Jerusalem and waiting for the Holy Spirit. They were 120 people altogether.**

While they waited, they prayed together. They waited for ten days until the Day of Pentecost had come. Pentecost was the feast day when the people of Israel thanked God for the first fruit of their crops.

The Bible shows us that the Holy Spirit came to the believers early on Pentecost morning. First there was a sound from heaven like a great wind. Then something like fire appeared on each of the 120 believers who were praying together. Immediately the believers began to praise God in languages which the Holy Spirit gave them. All of this showed that the Holy Spirit had come, just as Jesus the Messiah had promised.

Hundreds of people came to see and hear what was happening. At this time Jerusalem was a great city with people from many countries living there. Also many people had come to Jerusalem to worship during the Passover Feast and the Day of Pentecost.

When people heard the believers, they were very surprised, because each person heard the believers telling the wonderful works of God in his own language! For example: Arabians heard the message in Arabic. Greeks heard the message in Greek. This was a sign that God calls people by his Spirit from every nation into the church (Acts 2:1-13).

Soon the disciple Peter stood up and began to preach. He carefully showed the people that Jesus had completed what the prophets had told about the Messiah. He explained that Jesus is indeed the Messiah who gave his life so people could be saved from their sins. Peter finished preaching by calling out, "All the people of Israel, then, are to know for sure that this Jesus, whom you crucified, is the one that God has made Lord and Messiah" (Acts 2:36).

When the people heard this, they realised that what Peter said was true and asked him and the other disciples, "What shall we do, brothers?" (Acts2:37).

Peter answered, "Each one of you must turn away from his sins and be baptised in the name of Jesus Christ, so that your sins will be forgiven; and you will receive God's gift, the Holy Spirit" (Acts 2:38).

That day about 3,000 people believed and were baptised! That was the beginning of the Church.

## Practices of the Church

The disciples baptised everyone who repented of his sins and believed in the Messiah. Baptism has always been a Christian practise which has deep meaning.

---

**Remember:** John the Baptist baptised people with water in the Jordan River as a sign that they had repented of their sins. Before Jesus went to heaven he told his disciples to baptise all believers in "the name of the Father, and the Son, and the Holy Spirit" (Matthew 28:19).

For this reason the leaders of the Church baptise with water those who repent and believe in Jesus the Messiah. Baptism shows that a person has joined the Church.

---

The people of the Church in Jerusalem listened to the teachings of the disciples every day. The believers worshipped God with joy. As they worshipped, they shared bread and a cup of drink with each other. This was communion.

> **Remember:** When Jesus had his last Passover feast with his disciples, he broke bread and shared it with them. He also shared a cup of drink with them. The broken bread and the shared cup were a sign that Jesus the Messiah gave his life so that our sins can be forgiven.
>
> For this reason, Christians often share bread and a cup of drink together in worship. This is called Communion or the Lord's Table. It reminds the Church that Jesus the Messiah gave his life for the forgiveness of sins.

The believers shared their possessions with each other because they loved one another. The Bible says: "All the believers continued together in close fellowship and shared their belongings with one another. They would sell their property and possessions, and distribute the money among all, according to what each one needed" (Acts 2:44-45).

The people of Jerusalem could see that God was with the Church because the disciples healed people and did many other signs. The Bible says: "Many miracles and wonders were done through the apostles, and everyone was filled with awe*" (Acts 2:43).

### The Story of Saul (Acts 9:1-22)

Soon trouble came to the believers. Saul was a Jewish religious leader in Jerusalem, and he hated the Church. He thought that all Christian believers were turning people away from God. For this reason Saul tried to kill the Christian believers. He put many of them in prison.

Because of this persecution, many believers left Jerusalem. They went to other cities and other countries. Later some of them went to Africa, Europe, and far east into Asia. Wherever the believers went, they told people about Jesus the Messiah. Soon new Churches were beginning in all the countries around Palestine. One of these new Churches was in the city of Damascus in Syria.

Saul decided to go to Damascus to persecute the Christian believers in that city. On the way to Damascus, a bright light shone out of heaven. Saul fell to the ground in fear. Then a voice called, "Saul! Saul! Why do you persecute me?"(Acts 9:4).

Saul answered, "Who are you, Lord?" (Acts 9:5).

The voice said, "I am Jesus, whom you persecute" (Acts 9:5).

When Saul got up from the ground, he could not see. The light had made him blind. The men who were with him guided him into Damascus.

7

When Saul got to Damascus, God sent one of the Christian believers named Ananias to him. Ananias prayed for him, and then Saul could see again. Then Saul was baptised as a sign that he was a believer in Jesus the Messiah. Later Ananias brought Saul to the Church in Damascus. They accepted him.

## The Church on Earth

The Church has always been a growing fellowship of believers. Today this wonderful fellowship is found in nearly every country on earth.

---

**Remember:** In the Old Testament we learned that God made a covenant with the People of Israel at Mount Sinai when he gave them the Ten Commandments. Circumcision was a sign that the people had accepted God's covenant. But the People of Israel broke their covenant with God by turning away from God.

In the New Testament we learn that God created a New People of the Covenant. God created the New People of the Covenant through the work of Jesus the Messiah. Baptism is a sign that people have accepted God's New Covenant.

The Old Covenant with the People of Israel was based on the Ten Commandments and right worship in the tabernacle. The Old Covenant was a sign to prepare the world for a new and better covenant.

The New Covenant is based on the life, death and resurrection of Jesus the Messiah. Everyone who believes in the Messiah is in fellowship with the new people of God who are called the Church.

---

The things which God did when he first began to call people into the Church are important. They are signs from God which help us understand what the Church really is.

Here is a list of nine truths that these signs from God show us about the Church.

1. **The Church is a believing fellowship.** The Church is all the people who have heard and obeyed God by believing in Jesus the Messiah.

   Once Jesus asked his disciples, "Who do you say I am?"

   The disciple Peter answered, "You are the Messiah, the Son of the living God."

   Jesus replied, "Good for you, Simon son of John! For this truth did not come to you from any human being, but it was given to you directly by my Father in heaven" (Matthew 16:16, 17).

   This shows that it was God who called Peter to believe in Jesus the Messiah. God calls people everywhere to believe in Jesus the Messiah. The Church is made up of the people who have obeyed God's call to receive Jesus the Messiah.

2.  **The Church has many local fellowships**, which are part of the whole worldwide fellowship. Wherever the believers at a certain place meet together for worship, they are a local Church. When many believers come together for worship, that is a large local Church. When a few meet, they are a small Church.

    But the believers around the world are part of the world-wide Church. All the local churches belong to the world-wide Church. The Bible says that people "from every tribe, language, nation and race" (Revelation 5:9) belong to the world-wide Church.

3.  **The Church is a special unity.** Although there are many different Christian groups, the world-wide Church is a special kind of unity. The Bible says: "There is one body (Church) and one Spirit, just as there is one hope to which God has called you. There is one Lord, one faith, one baptism; there is one God and Father of all mankind who is Lord of all, works through all, and is in all" (Ephesians 4:4- 6)

4.  **The Church is a fellowship which worships.** The Bible says that when the Church began, the Christians "spent their time in learning from the apostles, taking part in the fellowship, and sharing in the fellowship meals and the prayers" (Acts 2:42)

5.  **The Church is a witnessing fellowship.** Jesus said: "But when the Holy Spirit comes upon you, you will be filled with power, and you will be witnesses for me in Jerusalem, in all Judea and Samaria, and to the ends of the earth" (Acts 1:8). The Church is to tell people throughout the world the good news that the Messiah from God has come.

6.  **The Church is a sharing and a serving fellowship.** Jesus said: "My commandment is this: Love one another, just as I have loved you" (John 15:12). At another place the Bible says: "We should do good to everyone, and especially to those who belong to our family in the faith" (Galatians 6:10). We know that as soon as the Church began, the believers began to share their possessions with those who were in need.

7.  **The Church is an obedient fellowship.** The Bible says: "…the church submits itself to (obeys) Christ" (Ephesians 5:24).

8.  **The Church is a suffering fellowship.** Jesus said: "But I chose you from this world, and you do not belong to it; that is why the world hates you" (John 15:19).

9.    **The Church is a victorious fellowship.** Jesus said: "I will build my church, and not even death will ever be able to overcome it" (Matthew 16:18). Sometimes the world recognises the true love of God because of the suffering service of the Church.   For this reason even persecution cannot defeat the Church.

**Remember:** You can see the Church whenever people meet together for worship in the name of Jesus the Messiah.  The Messiah himself is always present in the Church through the Holy Spirit.   Jesus said: "For where two or three come together in my name, I am there with them" (Mathew 18:20).

---

**Here is a difficult word in this Lesson.**

Awe          -          fear

---

**Learn this verse.** It gives an important idea in the lesson.

Ephesians 4:4-6: "There is one body and one Spirit, just as there is one hope to which God has called you.   There is one Lord, one faith, one baptism; there is one God and Father of all mankind, who is Lord of all, works through all, and is in all."

**Notice**

Now turn to the lesson tests in the back of the book and write answers for Lesson One.  Do the same for each of the other lessons after you have studied them.

# Lesson 2

## The Bible

Before you do this lesson, read these verses from the Bible: 2 Timothy 3:10-17

Acts 26:1-32

Now read the lesson and do the test at the end. The lesson explains what you have read in the Bible.

---

Just before Jesus the Messiah returned to heaven, he promised his disciples: "But when the Holy Spirit comes upon you, you will be filled with power, and you will be witnesses for me... to the ends of the earth" (Acts 1:8).

Some of Jesus' disciples found that a good way to be a witness was to write books about the life and teaching of the Messiah. For this reason four books were written about the life of the Messiah, and these books are called the Injil.

Other followers of the Messiah wanted to explain more about Jesus' teachings, so they wrote more books. These books are often called letters or Epistles. The man who wrote the largest number of books in the New Testament was Paul.

### Paul Was a Witness

Paul was one of the great witnesses in the Church. Before Paul believed in the Messiah, he persecuted the Christians. At that time he was called Saul. But when Saul heard the voice of the Messiah, he became a different man. He began to love people instead of hating them. They called him Paul instead of Saul. Paul means the little one. Perhaps they called him Paul because he became humble instead of proud.

Later Paul witnessed about Jesus the Messiah in other countries. He travelled to the lands that are now called Turkey and Greece. Everywhere he went, he preached about Jesus the Messiah. God blessed the witness of Paul and many Jews and Greeks believed in the Messiah. Many local Churches began through Paul's witness.

This made some of the Jewish religious leaders angry. They thought Paul was turning the people from God. Once when Paul was visiting Jerusalem these leaders caught Paul and had him put in prison. Later Paul was sent to prison in Rome where he was kept for many months.

### Letters to the Churches

While Paul was travelling and while he was in prison, Paul wrote many letters. Some of Paul's letters were to his friends and leaders in the Church. Other letters explained to the Christians the truth of the Gospel. In some letters Paul wrote about things that were wrong in the churches he had started. In all of these letters Paul explained the meaning of the life and teachings of the Messiah.

Some other disciples, such as John and Peter, also wrote letters. Each of these letters is a witness about Jesus the Messiah. The Holy Spirit guided these men as they wrote these letters.

The Christians knew that these writings were God's special message to the Church, and so the Church chose many of these letters to be included in the New Testament. We have already said that these letters are called the Epistles. The names of the Epistles usually show to whom they were first sent. For example, the New Testament Epistle called Romans, was a letter from Paul to the Church at Rome.

---

**Remember:** The Bible has two parts. The Old Testament was written before Jesus the Messiah came. The New Testament was written after the Messiah came.

The Old Testament contains the five books of the Taurat of the Prophet Moses and the Zabur of the Prophet David. The Old Testament also contains other books of prophecy and history. The books of the Old Testament were written in the Hebrew language.

The New Testament contains the four books of the Injil. It also contains the book of Acts which is a history of the early church. Then there are the Epistles which are letters from some of the disciples.

---

The writers of the Bible were guided by the Holy Spirit of God as they wrote. The Bible says: "All scripture is inspired* by God and is useful for teaching the truth, rebuking* error, correcting faults, and giving instruction for right living" (2 Timothy 3:16). For this reason all the books of the Old Testament and New Testament are God's own message to mankind.

### Christians Respect the Bible

The true message of the Bible is that Jesus the Messiah came from God, lived among people, gave his life on the cross as the perfect sacrifice for sin, and rose from the dead (1 Corinthians 15:3-4).

The Bible says: "In the past, God spoke to our ancestors many times in many ways through the prophets; but in these last days he has spoken to us through his Son (the Messiah)" (Hebrews 1:1-2). The New Testament shows that Jesus is the Messiah whom the prophets of the Old Testament wrote about and hoped for. For this reason we need the whole Bible in order to understand God's full message to mankind.

Christians believe that all the writings of the Bible are from God. For this reason Christians respect these writings greatly.

> The Quran also shows great respect for all the Scriptures which have been revealed by God. Surat Al-Ma'idah (5) ayah 68 says: "O people of the Book, you have nothing to stand upon until you establish the Taurat and the Injil and that which was revealed to you from your Lord."

God often warned the people not to change anything which the prophets and other writers had written. One of these warnings is found at the end of the New Testament. "I warn everyone who hears the prophetic words of this book: If anyone adds anything to them, God will add to his punishment the plagues described in this book. Or if anyone takes anything away from the prophetic words of this book, God will take away from him his share of the fruit of the tree of life and of the Holy City, which are described in this book" (Revelation 22:18-19).

The first Christians knew that they must guard every word of the Bible with great care. They also knew that people everywhere should read the Bible. For this reason they copied the books of the Bible again and again. These copies were sent to churches everywhere. Today we have about 5,000 early copies of parts of the New Testament. These copies prove that the men who copied the New Testament were careful not to make mistakes.

## The Bible Translated into Many Languages

At first the New Testament was written only in the Greek language. But soon churches appeared in countries where people did not know the Greek language. For this reason Christians translated* the New Testament and then the whole Bible into the language of the people. For example, about 1,600 years ago Egyptian Christians translated the Bible into four of the Egyptian languages. They did this so that all Egyptians could read God's word in their own languages.

Many years later the English people heard the Good News of Jesus the Messiah. About 600 years ago the English Christians translated the Bible into the English language. Today there are many English translations of the Bible. Some of these translations are in simple English, and some are difficult English.

About 100 years ago Christians in East Africa translated the Bible into the Swahili language. Today the Bible has been translated into most of the languages of Africa. The Hausa, Somalis, Arabs, Nubians, all have the Bible in their own language. Millions of Africans can now read the Bible in their mother tongue.

All these Bibles are translations of early copies of the Hebrew Old Testament and the Greek New Testament.

It is the will of God that people everywhere hear the truth of God which is revealed in the Bible. The Bible says: "God our Saviour...wants everyone to be saved and to come to know the truth" (1 Timothy 2:4). It is through the Bible that we learn to know of Jesus the Messiah who came from God.

---

**Here is a list of difficult words in this lesson.**

Inspired    -    caused

Rebuking    -    telling someone to stop doing wrong

Instruction    -    teaching

Translated    -    to change from one language to another.

---

**Learn this verse.** 2 Timothy 3:16: "All scripture is inspired by God and is useful for teaching the truth, rebuking error, correcting faults, and giving instruction for right living."

# Lesson 3

## The Way of Righteousness

Before you do this lesson, read these verses from the Bible: Matthew 5:1-48
Matthew 6:1-34
Matthew 7:1-28

Now read the lesson and do the test at the end.  The lesson explains what you have read in the Bible.

---

We often wonder, "What is the right thing to do?"  We all need to know how we should live.  We need to know what the will of God really is.

Once the religious leaders asked Jesus the Messiah to explain to them what the will of God is.  They asked him which commandment from God is the greatest.

Jesus answered: "Love the Lord your God with all your heart, with all your soul, and with all your mind.  This is the greatest and most important commandment.  The second most important commandment is like it: Love your neighbour as you love yourself.  The whole Law of Moses and the teachings of the prophets depend on these two commandments" (Matthew 22:37-40).

This teaching from Jesus the Messiah shows that it is God's will that we love God and people.  All God's rules for right living are based on the way of love.

### Teaching on a Mountain

One day when Jesus the Messiah was still living on the earth, he took his disciples up a mountain.  The mountain was in the country of Galilee which was where Jesus lived when he was a young boy.  Many people climbed the mountain to see and hear the Messiah.

Jesus sat on the mountain and began to teach his disciples.  He explained God's rules for right living which are based on the way of love.

### The Way of Blessing (Mathew 5:1-20)

"Happy are those who know they are spiritually poor; the Kingdom of heaven belongs to them!" (Mathew 5:3).  This is the first thing Jesus the Messiah told his disciples on the mountain.

This truth is most important.  The Kingdom of heaven is present whenever people live in true righteousness and love.  But only people who are poor in spirit enter God's kingdom of righteousness.

15

People who are poor in spirit are not proud. They know that they are sinful. They admit their sin. They accept the forgiveness of God. They experience the new life which comes through Jesus the Messiah. This new life is given by the power of God's Spirit within a person which helps him to live righteously.

### The Laws of God (Matthew 5:17-20)

Remember the Ten Commandments which God revealed through the Prophet Moses. Remember the writings of the prophets of God in the Old Testament. The Messiah did not come to put away the teachings of these prophets. Jesus the Messiah reveals the true and deep meaning of the laws and teachings of God which are written in the Old Testament.

Jesus said, "I have not come to do away with them, but to make their teaching come true" (Matthew 5:17).

Some religious people think that they are doing the will of God because they try to obey many different rules which the prophets have given. It is not wrong to obey these rules. Yet God's greatest commandment is that we love God most of all, and that we love other people.

If we think that we are obeying the laws of God, but do not show love, then we are not really doing the will of God. That is why Jesus warned people not to love like the religious leaders in his time. These men carefully obeyed the religious laws, but they did not love others.

This is the reason Jesus said: "You will be able to enter the kingdom of heaven only if you are more faithful than the teachers of the Law and the Pharisees in doing what God requires" (Matthew 5:20).

### Peace (Matthew 5: 21-26)

God told the Prophet Moses: "You shall not kill."

But Jesus the Messiah revealed that even the hate which leads people to kill is wrong. Jesus said: "But now I tell you: whoever is angry with his brother will be brought to trial" (Matthew 5:22).

A person cannot worship God truthfully if he does not have peace with his brother. First we must make peace with the one who is against us. Then we can worship with joy.

### Marriage (Matthew 5:27-32)

At Mount Sinai God told the people of Israel: "You shall not commit adultery." Jesus the Messiah revealed that even the desire for a woman who is not one's wife is sin. Jesus said: "But now I tell you: anyone who looks at a woman and wants to posses her is guilty* of committing adultery with her in his heart" (Matthew 5: 28).

16

Jesus the Messiah showed that adultery is a great evil. He said that if a part of our bodies such as the eye, tempts us, it would be better to have the eye taken out than to yield to temptation. He said: "It is much better for you to lose a part of your body than to have your whole body thrown into hell" (Matthew 5: 29).

Jesus the Messiah also explained that divorce is wrong. Jesus said: "But now I tell you: if a man divorces his wife, unless she has been unfaithful, then he is guilty of making her commit adultery if she marries again; and the man who marries her commits adultery also" (Matthew 5:32).

---

**Remember**: When God brought Eve to Adam, Adam said, "Bone taken from my bone, and flesh from my flesh." Then God revealed that when a man and a woman marry "they become one flesh" (Genesis 2:24). This shows that when a man and a woman marry, God himself makes them one in a special way.

Jesus said: "Man must not separate, then, what God has joined together" (Matthew 19:6). Jesus explained that the Prophet Moses permitted divorce because people were not willing to obey God's perfect will. But from the beginning of the world it is clear that it is against the will of God for a husband and wife to divorce each other (Matthew 19: 8).

When a husband and wife divorce, they destroy the marriage which God has joined. In the same way, the special oneness which God created in marriage is spoiled if a man marries two or more wives.

---

God's plan for marriage is that one man and one woman should live together in unity and faithfulness as long as they both live.

### Truthfulness (Matthew 5:33-37)

Jesus the Messiah told the disciples to be truthful. Disciples of Jesus should not need to swear* to prove they are telling the truth. A simple "yes" or "no" should be enough for one who is truthful.

### Forgiveness (Matthew 5: 38-48)

Some teachers say, "An eye for an eye and a tooth for a tooth." This means that if someone does something wrong to you, you should do the same thing to him.

But Jesus the Messiah taught that we should not stop the one who does wrong to us. If anyone hits us on the right cheek, we should let him hit the left cheek also. If anyone takes our coats, we should let him have our shirts also. If anyone forces us to carry his loads one kilometre, we should carry it for two kilometres.

Some people say, "You should love your neighbour and hate your enemy."

17

But Jesus the Messiah said that we should love our enemies and pray for those who persecute us. Jesus reminded us that God is kind both to the evil people and the good. If we love only those who love us, we are no different than the evil people. Even wicked people do good to their friends.

Love is more powerful than hate. If a person hates his enemy, the hate between them grows. Probably they will fight. Perhaps they will destroy each other. But a person should love and forgive his enemy. If he does this, it is possible that his enemy will become his friend.

The disciples of Jesus should love and be kind to both their friends and their enemies.

### Religious Acts (Matthew 6: 1-18)

Jesus the Messiah taught that we should not do our religious acts so as to get honour from men. When we give gifts to the poor, we should not tell others what we have done. God knows what we have done and will bless us for our gifts. That is a great reward. When we pray we should not try to get the attention of people. Instead we should go to our room and shut the door and pray there to God. When we go without food for religious reasons, we should not do this to show others that we are hungry. God, who always sees us, will bless us. The blessing of God is far better than the praises of men.

Jesus the Messiah said that when we pray, we should not use many useless words like unbelievers do. We should pray simple prayers something like this.

> "Our Father in heaven,
> May your holy name be honoured;
> May your kingdom come;
> May your will be done on earth as it is in heaven.
> Give us today the food we need.
> Forgive us the wrong that we have done just as we forgive the
> wrongs that others have done to us.
> Do not bring us to hard testing, but keep us safe from the evil one"
> (Matthew 6:9-13).

Jesus the Messiah also reminded us that if we forgive others the wrongs they have done to us, God will also forgive us for our wrongs. But if we do not forgive those who have wronged us, God will not forgive us for our sins.

### Riches (Matthew 6:19-34)

Jesus the Messiah also taught that all the riches in the world will become old and useless sometime. So we should not gather for ourselves these riches. Instead we should save up riches in heaven where riches never lose their value.

A person cannot serve God and money. So we should not trouble ourselves with money and the other things that money buys. God knows what we need. He will take care of us. The most important thing for us should be the Kingdom of God and the way God wants us to live. If we do that, all the things we need will be given to us. We should never worry about the future! God will take care of us.

*Jesus taught that we should be kind and truthful*

### Kindness (Matthew 7: 1-12)

Jesus the Messiah said: "Do not judge others, so that God will not judge you" (Matthew 7:1). Before we tell friends that they have done something wrong, we should look at ourselves because we also do wrong. We should first repent of our own sins. Only then can we help someone else repent of his sins. If we judge others unkindly, they will do the same to us.

God never judges unkindly. In fact he answers prayers and gives us good things. We should be kind to others.

Jesus said: "Do for others what you want them to do for you: this is the meaning of the Law of Moses and of the teachings of the prophets" (Matthew 7:12). This saying of Jesus is called the Golden Rule.

## Heaven and Hell (Matthew 7:13-23)

Jesus the Messiah said: "Go in through the narrow gate, because the gate to hell is wide and the road that leads to it is easy, and there are many who travel it. But the gate to life is narrow and the way that leads to it is hard, and there are a few people who find it" (Matthew 7: 13-14). This saying of Jesus shows that only a few people choose the straight road to heaven. Most people prefer the wide road to hell.

Many people say they obey, but they show by their actions that they do not love God or other people. These people are false. They will be sent away from God on the Day of Judgement. Speaking of these people, Jesus said: "And any that does not bear good fruit is cut down and thrown into the fire" (Matthew 7:19).

## The Foolish and the Wise (Matthew 7:24-27)

Jesus the Messiah finishes this lesson by telling a story to show what happens to a person who obeys his teaching and to a person who does not obey his teaching.

Jesus the Messiah said, "So then, anyone who hears these words of mine and obeys them is like a wise man who built his house on the rock. The rain poured down, the rivers overflowed, and the wind blew hard against that house. But it did not fall, because it was built on rock.

"But anyone who hears these words of mine and does not obey them is like a foolish man who built his house on sand. The rain poured down, the rivers overflowed, the wind blew hard against that house, and it fell. And what a terrible fall that was!" (Matthew 7: 24-27)

When Jesus finished saying these things, the crowd was amazed at the way he taught. He wasn't like the teachers of the Law; instead, he taught with authority" (Matthew 7: 28-29).

---

**Here is a list of difficult words in this lesson.**

| | | |
|---|---|---|
| Guilty | - | when someone does wrong he is guilty |
| Swear | - | to promise something in the name of God |
| Amazed | - | greatly surprised |

---

**Learn this verse.** Matthew 7: 12: "Do for others what you want them to do for you."

# Lesson 4

## Blessing through the Messiah

Before you do this lesson, read these verses from the Bible: Hebrews 4:14-16
Hebrews 7:23-25
Hebrews 10:11-14
Hebrews 10: 21-23

Now read the lesson and do the test at the end. The lesson explains what you have read in the Bible.

What is the Messiah doing now? We have learned that Jesus the Messiah returned to heaven after rising from the dead. What is he doing in heaven? Is he resting? No indeed!

God sent Jesus the Messiah to be our priest, prophet, and king (Hebrew 4:15). In this lesson we shall study the work of Jesus as our priest. The priestly work of Jesus the Messiah means that he is our helper. If we believe in him, we will receive blessings from God.

### The Work of a Priest

Aaron was the first high priest of the People of Israel. Aaron's sons were also priests. Aaron the high priest helped the people in many ways. He made animal sacrifices for the sins of the people and prayed to God for the people. He also led the people in worship and offered gifts of thanksgiving to God for the people.

But Aaron could never be a perfect priest because Aaron was not a perfect man. In fact, he made the golden calf for the People of Israel to worship. And Aaron died like all men do. After Aaron died, his work as priest was finished. Other men took his place.

### God Sent the Messiah to be Priest Forever

But God had a better plan. God wanted all people to have a perfect priest who would serve us forever. That perfect priest is Jesus the Messiah.

God chose the Messiah to be our perfect priest before the world began (1 Peter 1:18-20). The Bible says: "Christ did not take upon himself the honour of being a priest. Instead, God said to him... 'You will be a priest forever'" (Hebrews 5:5-6).

Here are five ways that we know Jesus the Messiah is our perfect high priest:

1. The Messiah was sent by God to live among people. For this reason the Messiah can understand us. He knows how difficult life is for us (Hebrews 2:17).
2. The Messiah lived a perfect life. He showed that we do not have to sin. His life is the perfect example for us to follow (Hebrews 4:15).

3. The Messiah was filled with grace, mercy and power (Hebrews 4:16). When he lived on earth, he healed the sick, and helped the poor in a wonderful way.

4. The Messiah gave his life on the cross as the perfect sacrifice for our sins (Hebrew 10:11-14).

5. The Messiah rose from the dead. He lives with God in heaven (Hebrews 7:23- 25).

No other priest was ever filled with grace and power like the Messiah. No one except the Messiah has given his life on the cross and risen from the dead. Only the Messiah can be our perfect high priest.

## The Work of the Messiah as Priest

Jesus the Messiah is our perfect high priest. He works in the world today through the Holy Spirit. The work of the Messiah is to help us. Here are four ways in which the Messiah helps us today.

1. **The Messiah saves us from our sins.** Whenever we ask God to forgive us, God does forgive us because the Messiah gave his life for us (Hebrews 7: 25-27).

2. **The Messiah gives us power over sin and Satan**. Whenever we ask God to help us turn from temptations, the Messiah also asks God to help us. The Messiah understands us and helps us because he also has lived among people. For this reason he understands us perfectly, and he asks God to help us so that we can have strength to turn away from sin and live righteously (Hebrews 7:25).

3. **The Messiah gives us power over Satan and evil spirits.** We know that Satan tries to bring evil into our lives and our homes. There are many evil spirits (Jinn) who help Satan do his evil work. These evil spirits often trouble people and they bring fear into our lives.

   Jesus the Messiah is greater than Satan and all the evil spirits. Therefore we can trust the Messiah to send away Satan and all the evil spirits from us. The evil spirits always go away when we put our trust in Jesus the Messiah. The Messiah himself has promised that in his name we shall cast out the evil spirits (Mark 16: 17).

4. **The Messiah brings us grace and blessing (baraka) from God.** Whenever we pray to God in the name of the Messiah, God answers. Through the Messiah, God gives us comfort and help when we are unhappy, afraid, sick, or helpless. He gives us strength in our time of need (Hebrews 4:16).

5. **The Messiah brings us into the presence of God.** Jesus the Messiah brings all believers into fellowship with God the Father. He opens the way for us to come to God without fear. The Bible says: "We have a great high priest in charge of the house of God (the church). So let us come near to God with a sincere* heart and a sure faith" (Hebrews 10:21-22).

## Keeping on the Way

Christians often speak of the Christian life as The Way (Acts 9:2). The Way is the way of love. It is also the way of blessing. We need to be careful because it is easy to leave The Way. Satan, people who are not believers, and our own desire for sin can lead us from The Way. For this reason we need help.

Here are four suggestions to stay on The Way:

1. Read the Bible and pray to God every day.

2. Tell other people the Good News of Jesus the Messiah.

3. Worship with other Christians often. They can advise you, pray with you, and give the encouragement you need. The Bible says: "Let us be concerned for one another to show love and to do good. Let us not give up the habit of meeting together, as some are doing. Instead, let us encourage one another all the more since you see that the Day of the Lord is coming near" (Hebrew 10: 24-25).

4. When you are tempted to sin, ask God for power to turn from the temptation. If you do sin, ask God to forgive you. Remember that God has appointed Jesus the Messiah to be your helper so that you can have power to stay in The Way.

---

**Remember:** A person begins the Christian Way through faith in Jesus the Messiah. He also continues in The Way through faith in the Messiah whom God has sent. The Bible says: "Since you have accepted Christ Jesus as Lord, live in union with him, build your lives on him, and become stronger in your faith, as you were taught. And be filled with thanksgiving" (Colossians 2:6, 7).

---

**Here is a difficult word in this lesson.**

Sincere        -        true

---

**Learn this verse.** Hebrews 7:25: "And so he is able, now and always, to save those who come to God through him, because he lives forever to plead with God for them."

# Lesson 5

## The Day of Judgement

Before you do this lesson, read these verses from the Bible: Revelation 5:9-14

Revelation 20:11-15

Revelation 21:1-8

Revelation 21:1-5

Now read the lesson and do the test at the end.   The lesson explains what you have read in the Bible.

---

Trouble is increasing everywhere in the world.   People are afraid.   We wonder what will happen next.   We wish we could find a way to stop trouble.

The Bible says that trouble will keep increasing until the Day of Judgement (Matthew 24:3-13).   At the Day of Judgement the world will be destroyed, and a new heaven and a new earth will be made.   God's Holy City which he has made in heaven will come down to earth.   The Holy City will be filled with the love of God.

God has revealed some things to us about the Day of Judgement.   Much of the last book in the Bible is about the coming of God's Holy City and the Day of Judgement.   This book is called Revelation.   The disciple John wrote the book of Revelation.   God revealed the truths in Revelation to John when he was a very old man.   John wrote what God showed him about the future of the world.

### The Messiah is Judge (Revelation 5:9-14)

In the book of Revelation we read that God has appointed Jesus the Messiah to be judge at the Day of Judgement (2 Corinthians 5:10; Revelation 5:5).   The heavenly beings will be very happy when they learn that the Messiah is the Judge.   They will sing a great song of praise to the Messiah saying something like this (Revelation 5:9-14):

You have the honour Jesus,
because you gave your life in sacrifice
so that people were saved from sin for God
from every people on earth,
and you have made these people become
the true people of God.

Other forms of heavenly and earthly life will praise the Messiah too. Many thousands of angels, all people both small and great, all animals, insects and birds will begin to praise God. Their voices of praise will grow louder and louder until the earth, sea and heavens will be filled with the praises of God. They will say: Jesus is worthy "to receive power, wealth, wisdom, strength, honour, glory and praise" (Revelation 5:12).

Everywhere in heaven and earth there will be joy because God has chosen the Messiah to be judge on the Day of Judgement.

## The Day of Judgement (Revelation 20:11-15)

Some day the Messiah will return to earth as Judge. When he comes, he will come quickly, like sudden light. The sun will turn black and the moon will look like blood. The stars will appear, and the sky will roll together like a great piece of paper. The earth will shake, the mountains will fall, and the islands will move.

The great people and the small, the rich and the poor, kings and the slaves, everyone who does not love God will run to the mountains and the holes in the ground to hide. They will cry, "Fall on us and hide us from the eyes of the one who sits on the throne" (Revelation 6:12-17).

All the people who have died since the beginning of the world will come out of the graves. They will all stand in front of the throne of judgement. Books will be brought before the judge, who is Jesus the Messiah. When the books are opened the judge will find in them the truth about every person. Nothing will be hidden that will not be made known at that time (Mark 4:22).

There will be another special book, which is the Book of Life. The Book of Life contains all the names of those whose sins have been forgiven. These have accepted the Messiah whom God sent into the world to save us from our sins.

Then the Messiah will make judgement (Matthew 25:34-41).

He will say to everyone whose name is found in the Book of Life: Come, you blessed of my Father, welcome to heaven which has been made ready for you.

But to those whose names are not found in the Book of Life, the Messiah will say: Go from me, you evil people, into the eternal fire which is made for Satan and his angels.

## God's Holy City (Revelation 21:1-8; 22:1-5)

At the Day of Judgement, the Holy City of God will appear. Those people whose names are found in the Book of Life will be with God in his Holy City.

There will be no more sorrow or pain in God's City. There will be no sun, for God himself will be the light of that Holy City. A tree of life and a river of life will be in the Holy City. There will be no more death.

We cannot understand now the full glory of God's Holy City. The Bible says' "What no one ever saw or heard, what no one ever thought could happen, is the very thing God prepared for those who love him."

But we know that God's Holy City, which is sometimes called heaven, will be a happy place because sin and evil will never enter there. God and all the people whose sins have been forgiven will be there.

## We Need to be Ready

All people everywhere who accept Jesus the Messiah as Saviour and Lord become the people of God on earth. On the Day of Judgement the Messiah will welcome the people of God into God's Holy City where they will live with God forever.

> We need to be ready (Revelation 22:20).
> The Messiah said: "Yes indeed! I am coming soon."
> The Church answers: "So be it. Come, Lord Jesus!"

---

# TESTS

Please write your name and address on the bottom of
the test and mail to:

# Test 1: The People of Faith

1. When the Messiah returned to heaven, his disciples
   - (a) went back to their homes in Galilee.
   - (b) immediately began to witness about Jesus.
   - (c) stayed in Jerusalem and waited for the Holy Spirit to come.                                   _____

2. On the day of Pentecost
   - (a) Jesus the Messiah returned to heaven.
   - (b) Jesus the Messiah was crucified.
   - (c) the Holy Spirit came upon Jesus' disciples.                                   _____

3. How many people believed and were baptised on the day of Pentecost?
   - (a) about 3,000
   - (b) about 1,000
   - (c) about 5,000                                   _____

4. Saul persecuted many
   - (a) Romans.
   - (b) Christians.
   - (c) Jewish leaders.                                   _____

5. On the road to Damascus
   - (a) Saul heard the voice of Jesus the Messiah.
   - (b) Saul met Ananias.
   - (c) Saul was baptised by Ananias.                                   _____

Write "True" or "False" after each of the following sentences.

6. All believers are part of the worldwide Church.                                   _____

7. The Holy Spirit gives the Church power to witness.                                   _____

8. The Church is a sharing fellowship.                                   _____

9. God does not let the Church suffer.                                   _____

10. The Church cannot be defeated.                                   _____

# Test 2: The People of Faith

1. The message of the Bible about Jesus the Messiah is
    - (a) only for Jews.
    - (b) only for Europeans.
    - (c) for all people everywhere.  _____

2. Saul's new name was
    - (a) Paul.
    - (b) Peter.
    - (c) John.  _____

3. The New Testament was first written
    - (a) in the Hebrew language.
    - (b) in the Greek language.
    - (c) in the English language.  _____

4. The letters in the New Testament are also called
    - (a) the Epistles.
    - (b) the Injil.
    - (c) the Zabur.  _____

5. When the Christians made copies of the Bible,
    - (a) they changed many things in the Bible.
    - (b) they destroyed all the older copies of the Bible.
    - (c) they were careful not to make mistakes.  _____

Write "True" or "False" after each of the following sentences.

6. The Old Testament was first written in the Hebrew language.  _____

7. Christians do not believe that the writings of the prophets
   are from God.  _____

8. God desires only a few people to be saved.  _____
9. God warned the people not to change what the prophets had written._____
10. The Bible has been translated into many languages.  _____

# Test 3: The People of Faith

1.  God's will for right living is based on
    - (a) the way of love.
    - (b) the way of sacrifice.
    - (c) the way of many rules and laws.           _____

2.  Jesus the Messiah
    - (a) put away the teachings of the prophets.
    - (b) taught people to hate their enemies.
    - (c) completed all that God revealed through
      the prophets.                                 _____

3.  Love is
    - (a) more powerful than hate.
    - (b) as powerful as hate.
    - (c) less powerful than hate.                  _____

4.  Jesus the Messiah taught that when we give gifts to the
    poor, we should
    - (a) tell many people.
    - (b) tell no one.
    - (c) tell only a few friends.                  _____

5.  "Whatever you wish that men would do to you, do so to
    them." This saying of Jesus is called
    - (a) the great commandment.
    - (b) the last law.
    - (c) the Golden Rule.                          _____

Write "True" or "False" after each of the following sentences.

6.  We all need to know how to live right.          _____
7.  People who are poor in spirit are proud.         _____
8.  Desire for a woman who is not your wife is sin.  _____
9.  It is against the will of God for a husband and wife to
    divorce each other.                             _____
10. We can serve God and money.                      _____

## Test 4:   The People of Faith

1.     Aaron could not be a perfect high priest because
    (a)   he was not a perfect man.
    (b)   he could not read the Taurat.
    (c)   he was a true son of Israel.                                _____

2.   The Messiah is our perfect high priest because
    (a)   he asked God to make him become our perfect priest.
    (b)   he came from the family of David.
    (c)   he was appointed to be our perfect priest by God.    _____

3.   A person begins the Christian way
    (a)   through giving to the poor.
    (b)   through baptism.
    (c)   through faith in Jesus the Messiah.                        _____

4.   A person continues in the Christian way
    (a)   through praying toward Jerusalem.
    (b)   through faith in Jesus the Messiah.
    (c)   through learning the Injil by memory.                     _____

5.   If we want to stay in the Christian way, we should
    (a)   never tell other people about Jesus the Messiah.
    (b)   never tell other people that we are Christians.
    (c)   tell other people the Good News of Jesus
          the Messiah.                                                       _____

Write "True" or "False" after each of the following sentences.

6.   Jesus the Messiah gave his life on the cross as the
     perfect sacrifice for our sins.                                    _____

7.   Jesus the Messiah can help us turn from sin and defeat Satan.    _____

8.   We should read the Bible and pray to God only once a week.    _____

9.   We should worship with other Christians often.              _____

10.  We should never admit that we sin.                            _____

# Test 5:   The People of Faith

1.   The Bible says that trouble
      (a)   will continue forever.
      (b)   will keep increasing until the Day of Judgement.
      (a)   was destroyed at the time of the Prophet Noah.     _____

3.   The last book of the Bible is called
      (a)   Matthew.
      (b)   Revelation.
      (c)   Judgement.     _____

4.   Whom has God appointed to be the judge at the Day of Judgement?
      (a)   Jesus the Messiah
      (b)   The Prophet Moses
      (c)   The Prophet Abraham     _____

5.   The Book of Life is written by
      (a)   the Prophet Moses.
      (b)   the Prophet David.
      (c)   Jesus the Messiah.     _____

5.   At the Day of Judgement
      (a)   all people, both good and evil, will be invited into heaven.
      (b)   all people who have accepted the Messiah will be invited
           into heaven.
      (c)   all people who give to the poor will be invited into
           heaven.     _____

Write "True" or "False" after each of the following sentences.

6.   God revealed the truths in Revelation to the disciple John.     _____

7.   Some day the Messiah will return to earth.     _____

8.   There will be sorrow in God's Holy City.     _____

9.   All people who accept Jesus the Messiah become the people
of God.     _____

10.   All people will live with God forever.     _____

The Bible shows us that God has chosen to reveal Himself to us and save us from our sin through the life, death and resurrection of the Messiah.

What do you believe about Jesus the Messiah?

The last verse in the Bible is a prayer of blessing (Revelation 22:21).

We offer the same prayer for you. This is our prayer: "The grace of the Lord Jesus be with you. Amen."

This is the Fourth and last course in the series called: **The People of God**
These are the four courses included in **The People of God** series:

**The Beginning of People**

**God's Covenant with People**

**God Loves People**

**The People of Faith**

### Consultants

| | |
|---|---|
| A. Ali | N. Idarous |
| J. Dahir | Y. Mohamed |
| H. Butler | P. Virts |
| D. Osman | P. Ipema |
| R. Hartzler | S. Mulatya |
| D. Shenk | |

### Acknowledgements

**The People of God** course is prepared for people who know the Quran, but who also want to know something about the Taurat of the Prophet Moses, the Zabur of the Prophet David, other Holy Writings of Prophets, and the Injil of Jesus the Messiah.

A variety of groups participated in preparing these courses. The Mennonite Board in Eastern Africa provided leadership to the writing team and contributed office facilities, finance, and personnel. World Outreach, Evangel Publishing House, Emmaeus School, and the Nairobi Baptist Church participated significantly. The Islam in Africa Project and the Area Committee of the National Christian Council of Kenya gave invaluable theological insights and counsel. The Department of Philosophy and Religious Studies of Kenyatta University College provided expertise and consultation. The World Association of Christian Communication contributed money for publishing the courses. Daystar Communications supervised pre-publication testing and revision. Several members of the Islamic community in Kenya evaluated the course and gave helpful suggestions for its development. The typing and editing were done by Naomi Smoker. Revisions for the second edition were made by Mennonite Islamic Ministries staff in Nairobi.

Made in the USA
Charleston, SC
02 December 2016